A Book of
Exquisite Disasters

THE PALMETTO POETRY SERIES

KWAME DAWES, SERIES EDITOR

Ota Benga under My Mother's Roof
Carrie Anne McCray, edited by Kevin Simmonds

A Book of Exquisite Disasters
Charlene Spearen

Seeking: Poetry and Prose Inspired by the Art of Jonathan Green
Edited by Kwame Dawes and Marjory Wentworth

A Book of
Exquisite Disasters

POEMS

Charlene Spearen

Foreword by Kwame Dawes

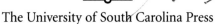

The University of South Carolina Press

Published in Cooperation with the South Carolina Poetry Initiative,
University of South Carolina

© 2012 University of South Carolina

Published by the University of South Carolina Press
Columbia, South Carolina 29208

www.sc.edu/uscpress

Manufactured in the United States of America

21 20 19 18 17 16 15 14 13 12   10 9 8 7 6 5 4 3 2 1

Library of Congress Cataloging-in-Publication Data

Spearen, Charlene Monahan.
   A book of exquisite disasters : poems / Charlene Spearen ;
foreword by Kwame Dawes.
      p. cm. — (The Palmetto poetry series)
   ISBN 978-1-61117-089-4 (pbk : alk. paper)
   I. Dawes, Kwame Senu Neville, 1962– II. Title.
   PS3619.P3737B66 2012
   811'.6—dc23

                                             2011052334

To John, Aimee, Alyse, and Christian

How can I reach your heart, you,
with a womb in your brain?

Agi Mishol,
Look There

Contents

Foreword

A Book of Exquisite Disasters is a splendid book of poetry.
Charlene Spearen's verse has that uncanny grace of being able
to engage very intimate and harrowing moments while finding
the language and the metaphors to make such moments reso-
nate even beyond their particular moment. Jon Anderson, in a
fascinating poem, "The Secret of Poetry," declared that the
secret of poetry "is cruelty," and in Spearen's poems she cap-
tures what Anderson is talking about. It is not that she (or
Anderson) indulges in that which is cruel, but that she faces
truths, faces them head on and with unwavering beauty retells
the truths whether they are painful or pleasant, and, in so
doing, she forces us to see. This is the cruelty that Anderson is
speaking of: a sweet and necessary cruelty. It takes such an
understanding of beauty and cruelty to write so harrowingly
and beautifully about, for example, the shock of abuse:

> I waver between the mirror and our lost
> childhood, and tilt my head, swallow
> stretched muscles, hold high a bottle of Visine,
>
> and question the need to see certain things.
> You have learned to fear darkness, and in
> an effort to climb out of your exhaustion,

you lift the night-hood. The sulfur-crested
cockatoo shrieks, fractures all eucharist-white
hope, godwit power, and catechism texts.

One of the most elegant sequences in the collection is a suite
of poems that form a beautiful elegy to her brother—nothing
maudlin or sentimental here, just a tough look at what made
him who he was and what made her love him and want to tell
stories of defiance, humor, and pathos. There is a grappling
with faith, fear, and family in these poems that is fresh and
engaging:

> Your body is so small, grows smaller
> each minute, your face bird-like.
> *No intervention.* Morphine drips silently
> and the drops tick through your last hours,
> delicately stitch this place and time.
> You wake, cough one word—*thirsty.*
> I tilt the glass, count three drops, your
> tongue curls, your parched lips move.
> These lines bright and swift rise: *Heaven
> is a place where minutes fold into eternity.
> Beauty made visible.* Perhaps *oblivion.*
>
> ("Fading")

The achievement of this sequence, however, is not so much
in how accurately she captures the complicated and touching
journey with death that she undergoes, but how this all-too-
real experience becomes transformed into beautiful poems—
lyrical explorations of such time-honored themes as loyalty,
fear, loss, and love—but, beyond that, wonderful studies in
how language, arresting experience, can produce these artifacts
of great and lasting beauty.

Throughout this collection we see Spearen throwing her
everything into the belief in poems, the belief in language,
the play, the leap and turn of images, the surprise of new

thoughts—ones that she might never have arrived at had she not embarked on a poem. That she manages to excite us with this sense of a discovery and surprise speaks to Spearen's abilities as a poet of craft and feeling. Observe the way the language leads her in this poem that becomes a veritable basket of delightful language and insight:

> In my village where the sweet sadness
> of truth waves its flag, we keep the dyer's
> secrets, guard them like delicacies,
> recipes that come from cracked mussels
> and fingered ink sacks. I tell the children,
> "Go, gather whortleberry, anchusa, black
> currant." We must make fast and bright
> colors—the lovely lavender, bristol red,
> gosling green, and mortal sin for queens,
> soldiers, and high-priests. At the day's end,
> I stir the pot, drown the spun, boiled yarn;
> and as I watch the piper play his tune, I dream
> another perfect-sounding, sad, new color.
> ("The Pot Stirrer")

Spearen has a staid eloquence about her syntax and language that reveals her studied sense of the line and how it must be shaped. But the obvious things can be said—and these things have to do with the themes that preoccupy Spearen. Her poetry is poetry about women, and for Spearen the sublime is distinctly presented in verse for women. She seems to be arguing that as women engage the world and allow themselves to reflect on their experience in the world, whether it is mothering, discovering and enjoying their sexuality, or grappling with the enslavement and liberation of faith, the path toward understanding comes through an engagement with the sublime—the rising about the mundane toward something beyond ourselves. In "I Used to Know My Name"—we are never asked to ignore the tragedy of the objectification of the woman's body, but we are also forced to hear her breath close to us—the revelation is all the more startling:

> But when Saarjite,
> later unwrapped and renamed *Hottentot*
>
> *Venus,* heard the luscious, vanilla
> ice cream *Come with me,* she filled
>
> her lush green world with an I-love-
> my-new-dress scream. Her Ken wore
>
> a bone-white lab coat, bone-white
> pants; his bone-white face sparked
>
> eyes blue as rolling waves. He pointed,
> twisted her head toward the great ship,
>
> said her world, top to bottom, would
> be transformed. He led her past the twiggy
>
> stuff of brush, past the men's sideways
> glance, up the plank, and when the last
>
> strip of land, the last fluency of color
> disappeared, he stripped her young girl
>
> body never saying her name, never saying
> *Saarjite,* only these two words: *Show me.*

I admire the open sensibility in Spearen—a sensibility open to influence, open to triggers from all sorts of places—whether it is a painting at the Columbia Museum of Art or a sculpting that opens the way for her to write a stunning celebration of life in a friend who is surviving cancer, or music, or the poems of other poets, or the ancient tales of Japanese courtesans. The list goes own, but what holds these poems together is the clear and assured voice of the poet—a poet blessed with chronological maturity, which has then allowed her to translate the wisdom of having living many lives, to the wisdom of poetic experience and understanding. We, quite simply, trust this voice for its honesty and humility:

> But I have
> entered death's space, a place less than agony;
> a time when urgency to move between this
> and that is not so far-reaching, have seen
> when the soul must turn, leave hindsight,
> follow the assigned path, it is veiled
> in a holy state and ceases to wonder about
> words like *blame* and *direction*.
>
> ("Judgment Day")

I have known Charlene Spearen for many years, and we have worked together as colleagues and coconspirators in the promotion and celebration of poetry in South Carolina. Yet our strongest connection has been around the discussion of poetry, the writing of poetry and the passion for what a poem can do. I have over the years become something of an editor who has worked with so many writers in bringing manuscripts to print. There are few such experiences in my life that match the pleasure with which I introduce the poetry of Charlene Spearen to readers. Apart from the pleasure that comes from seeing so many of these poems take shape over time and with revision, there is the greater pleasure of seeing many of these poems for the first time when Charlene Spearen finally pulled together her manuscript. I read the book with a mixture of satisfying familiarity and surprise and awe at the new work, at the work she has held back and shaped, at the new preoccupations, at the elegant architecture of the whole book.

This is a book of terrible and elegant beauty. It will reward constant reading. I am extremely happy that it is out there now. I am happier that it marks merely the beginning of what will be a career of many more books by Charlene Spearen that will be filled with surprise and beauty.

Acknowledgments

Grateful acknowledgement is owed to the following journals, literary magazines, and anthologies where some of the poems in this collection, or earlier versions of them, have appeared:

"Before the Peril of Unconsciousness" (an earlier version),
    in *Country Dog Review* (Winter 2010)
"The Pot Stirrer," in *Southern Poetry Anthology,* vol. 1, *South
    Carolina* (Texas Review Press, 2008)
"Midmorning Tea," in *Promise: Echoing the Artist Heart*
    (Spring/Summer 2003)
"Recounted Bliss," in *Writers at Carolina* (Spring 2002)
"The Nuns at St. Mary's," in *Aspect* (Spring 2000)
"Two Butterflies," in *Yemmassee* (Spring 1999)

A number of these poems appeared in earlier versions in my chapbook, *Without Processions* (Stepping Stone Press, 2006).

I

Magic inside a Hell-Box

Magic inside a Hell-Box

for C.J.M.

Morning. The early light centers
and fills the air like the smell
of new clothes on Easter Sunday.

You wear pajamas, soft flannel,
navy blue stripes and white piping
around the collar; something to cover

pallid veins that pulse against your
yellowed skin. You shield your eyes
from the shame of a shrinking body

and whistle to the hooded birdcage.
It hangs in the dark corner like a lost
thought that waits recognition.

We try to order the day, a longing,
a storming, a hope for a change in tactics
and say: *Good morning.* I wish I could

wage war, win the battle, keep the spirit
safe from the flesh; but the best we
can do is couch our battle cries inside

church hymns, prayers, and dead cold
acts of blasphemy. A need for reprieve.
Retreat is sometimes the best option.

I close the bedroom door, a momentary
R&R. The fluorescent light flickers.
Each day is a struggle for balance.

I waver between the mirror and our lost
childhood, and tilt my head, swallow
stretched muscles, hold high a bottle of Visine,

and question the need to see certain things.
You have learned to fear darkness, and in
an effort to climb out of your exhaustion,

you lift the night-hood. The sulfur-crested
cockatoo shrieks, fractures all eucharist-white
hope, godwit power, and catechism texts.

Perimeters

We crave the scent of summer sensations:
Short Beach, Long Island Sound, seagulls

circling, and haul our minds to the diving,
the music, the rush of morning tide.

We rewind the roll of darkening skies
and how the horseshoe crabs dug foxholes

how they separated seaweed strewn shores,
how gray pebbles rocked the blue-green water,

how we danced barefoot in the silt's swirl

while brackish waves gathered polished
ebony mussels, broken shells, curved spines,

splintered claws. Outside these pincered
memories, another confluence. I hug your

haggard body, pull tight the putrid green
of your army blanket, watch your son rub

and polish the brass that dots your hanging
uniform, and wonder, like a poem's line

surrendered for all to see, if these creatures,
their appearance like soldiers guarding borders,

were a reminder that all things labeled *living*
must, at some point, face approaching storms.

Eureka Street: Reviewed

One year ago,
mornings were a series
of false starts; days
an endless hammering of words, a constant
back and forth bantering.
You gave me a book, *Eureka Street*.

*"Read it, it will make you laugh; all the guys meet in a pub, say
'Fuck it' under a sign—An Evening of Irish Poetry—Tonight 8
P.M."* The dream always pleased you: green hillsides, Northern
Lights, a purple-gray dusk, a group called the Wild Geese. You
hummed their tune, lives fiercely set to a melody, called it a
luring song. The more you thought of places like Carrickatee
or Ballybay, the bogs, the turf, the dusty roads where ragged
men with flaming faces walked their tired asses, the further you
walked into your dream.

Now you are dying.
In the book, Belfast is a city
of jumbled streets, bumps in the road,
with only a whisper of God
and I say, "Let's travel to *Eureka Street*,

walk all the dark, lamp-lit alleys,
find that bar where they say,
'Fuck it,' play a tune, *Muddy Waters*—
maybe four times in a row."

Toward the Blue-White Moon

Order. Shaking our God-fist, we play
with simple arrangements: the couch,
it must go against this wall; the striped chair
in the corner, and the open-mouthed
fireplace (another must) in the room's
center. Always in a frenzied state, even
when we know life comes and goes
in zigzag patterns, we build daily lists.
Yours: *Live one more day.*

Drifting between here and now, you lie
sheeted in your blurred world, and deep
within the cavern of your body a moan
rises, and deep inside my blue-vein heart
this question pulsates: *How does one let go?*
A chaos only God and animals understand.

You are my loved-beyond-words brother,
and I have tried to challenge what is now
a must, like when I punched Billy Savage's
nose on the playground the third time he
pushed you. Or the time when I cradled
your young body, wept with your wounds
felt the sting after your wiry arms and legs
began to fly high like tossed confetti

from a sixteen-stair ladder. All children
want to hear they are king of the mountain.
Sometimes we just can't make it to the summit.

Outside, below a blue-white moon, the grass
is shrouded in gray mist, each dead accurate
blade, like you, lies still as if pressed inside
some secret diary, and with reckless prodigal
haste, I count the clock's migratory tic then toc
as if life and my love for you were a boxed
paint-by-number canvas: #1, leaf green; #2,
sky blue; #3, rose red; #4, our shared gardens—
a summer rainbow, a dazzling luster.

Your dog, its nose pressed against the slated
window, sees the room in softened Technicolor,
and with neither a thump nor thud tries to sniff
the air for your scent. She cries out with a soft yelp,
a sound like a child's whining; and without
so much as one look for reason or *why*,
or a need to resurrect a stockpile of regret,
this animal seems to know the cold, blue
landscape will empty, become a place
where you will never go again, and that
we all must go to the center of the end.

Take a Deep Breath

A familiar smell,
    Folgers. Your wife, hidden

in a vapor-cloud, cools
    the hot brown liquid.

Your breakfast (the most
    important meal):

extracts from a cod's liver,
    Italy's best olives,
dried seaweed, ginger
    au natural, a coffee enema.

Your wife says you
    still have time.

She visits her soothsayer,
    seeks his salvation recipes.

You say her hope is
    in the hands of Jesus

and a huckster—
    a seller of snake oil.

Out of Oncoming Darkness

There never was a need to be on the lookout
for angels, for life was a hell-box, a place
for peering, a poke here and there, a shuffle,
an adventurous ambling, and *direction*
was only a word. The world according to you
was a simple place, a concrete setting where
condemnation seldom wavered, maybe this
is why you always had so much loathing,
so much hot-tempered passion.

At Silverman's Horse Stables, you always
chose the Godless mare, climbed inside
those fiery eyes. Teuval tasted the wind,
vaulted down cold roads, nostrils flared,
galloped past the priest's white clapboard house;
together you illuminated winter light, swept
the December underpainting. *Heaven help
them,* my half prayer half admiration tossed
into the blue-white rising fury.

I will keep these images, box and label them.
Like the one I have of you lying in your hospital
bed (another unfolding), your body's temperature
racing higher, eyes frozen, silenced by the pulsing

search for some kind of hope, God or demon
sent. All is so fixed and heavy, and the only
thing racing now is my heartbeat and the chew
of cancer eating liver, kidneys, brain, trampling
the past, present, future and everything you loved.

Last Confession

It's been twenty-five years. Don't expect
me to tell each venial and mortal act,

how many times I lied, or went against
the rules, cursed a name, or drank too much.

Forget about the Masses missed, the times
I thought about killing my brother,

or wished my father was dead;
and we both know I could tell a few

real conversation stoppers; but
in the final hour of need when death

travels faster than any soul flying
out of purgatory, when we are feeling

empty like being homeless or helpless,
we speak simple words: I am more than

ashamed, or heartily sorry for all those sins
that hurt my neighbor, fractured my wife,

or slapped my children. I do believe
in Judgment Day, and if I could I'd go back,

swallow all the unholy desires. But for God's
sake before I float out wearing

a white suit of conditional penances, bless
me, Father, and my perfect Act of Contrition.

And of His Death

Propped up in bed, an arabesque of stick
limbs, bloated belly, and tangled sheets,
you give the death-ghost a kick. You have
given up measuring time with clocks, sun
or moon. The end is near; a moment when

one wing soars toward heaven while the other
sweeps the earth. We talk of St. Francis,
a holy man, a gentle man. You say he walked
with pain—imagine, day in, day out, as if iron
nails were driven deep inside each fleshy step.
You know this pain; it burns into bone
like a dying person's hope for release.

Another stab; your turn. This one knots,
cuts, then twists as you pull me to a whisper:
*Pain can move the body with the fervor
of sacred prayer.*

This morphine-slurred offering reminds me
how Francis would listen for the sound of flapping
wings, the Holy Spirit. I search for something
to do, something to say. Here is another picture.
A handful of poems stare their way into the darkening
room. I read one. Your glassy eyes clear, then tear.

You slowly move thumbtips to fingertips; I am
the acolyte as you extend your arms,
push forward these words: *Take my soul.*
And like those Franciscan brothers, heads lifted,
marching in procession, I want to lay you
on a stretcher and raise you high above
all that is torment and reason.

Fading

Your body is so small, grows smaller
each minute, your face bird-like.
No intervention. Morphine drips silently
and the drops tick through your last hours,
delicately stitch this place and time.
You wake, cough one word—*thirsty.*
I tilt the glass, count three drops, your
tongue curls, your parched lips move.
These lines bright and swift rise: *Heaven*
is a place where minutes fold into eternity.
Beauty made visible. Perhaps *oblivion.*
I turn your body doing what is *required.*
This last word comes in a soft murmur
as I sit beside your deathbed. I pray.
I watch, and inside your last lucid threshing,
my ear to your mouth, I hear how portals
can open: *Your reward awaits you in heaven.*

From Fort Mitchell Cemetery

There were doves wearing wings white
as communion veils, emissaries, cool
and calm, flowers in baskets, stargazer lilies,
offerings sent by those who lurked
like buzzards around your coffin—
a shimmering more than silver
that swallowed your ravaged body.
Yet I saw your temple as one gigantic
splinter, as broken bones, as lost prayer;
the god of good health, the one who could
heal, reshape, and nurture, was definitely out
so it seems. Circling, fluid as an eagle's
flight, the mourners passed the flag draped
dome. Funny, if you could, you would have
crowed: *Get out of here; find your own piece
of roadkill.* Six soldiers, like a team

of rowers, guards of grief wearing
khaki and brass, moved in unison.
They stood faceless as a pack of penguins;
buckles and buttons polished and rubbed
gleamed like a lightening-struck wave—
but never is a soldier taught how to talk
to the dead. I watched the group eye
each other, various phosphorescent agates.

And on cue, all bowed their heads then moved,
some two by two, across the cemetery-green
lawn. You would have thought each funeral
garbed man and woman was auditioning
for a part in some important play. But today,

only bit parts are available. Toward the end,
the men took turns shaking their heads
and your son's hand, saying things like,
You're the man of the house now—women
threw out their arms like some giant bird,
taking in your wife, hugging her like a lost
chick. A gaping hole in this snug nest.
Soldiers wheeled you from under the canopy,
two columns of obedience on either side.
The stage, stilled a second like sudden restraint, is yours.
Twenty-one bullets fly; the sound and smoke
float like feathers from a pheasant shot in flight.

II

Somehow She Found Herself

Somehow She Found Herself

for Barbara

And surely that girl one foot taller
and four years older who threatened
to hang me by my buckedtoothed smile
on the corner of Main and Monticello
like a head-drooped, lost-for-words,
pencil-drawn stick man would have
hesitated, and gaped, and swallowed
her wagging tongue. If only my longing
for acceptance, hanging like a loose
thread on the wind, could have pushed
me to reach for my star (yes, everyone
has one), pulled it down from hiding
behind the midday sun, felt its heavenly
burn, seen its brightness, letting just
a glimmer seep between middle and
ring finger, on that day I would have
grown an inch or two, would have seen
my power, and even stared at it in awe.

Mother of God

As if anyone can address
mayhem, the nun told me
to pray. But on that morning
my mother died, when the stars
and planets were no longer
assuredly on track, God hid
behind a stone-gray sky.

Cosmic disaster was everywhere:
a gambling father, two brothers,
one only five, my mother's room,
the deathbed, a wreckage dusted
with psalms and perfume.
Life was hardly worth a breath.

Trying to understand divine
interception, I entered St. Mary's
Chapel, a God-House, a hushed
place with a sacred dare-to-believe
language. I dabbed forehead,
bosom, and shoulders, inhaled
the holy water's fruit-sweet scent

then knelt before a lady whose veil
opened to eyes quiet as the sun's

coming. Never had I seen such
radiance fill alcove, aisle, pew.
And eased by the holy closeness,
of the statue's stone-white wrapping,
I began to feel heaven's omniscient

voice, the gold cross around my
neck, the Christ-Mother's extended
open palms, the elegant fingers undoing
all the loss
all the too hard to fathom
all the stone edgings
all that was His will
all that was God-sent.

In a Deep-Rooted Voice

You never easily get rid of it—
that place called *home,* and often

our homegrown stories come from
long days of self-contradiction.

Today, I enter this town's green scent
and feel the island's inlet breeze;

the rising emerald sweep knows,
like the onset of fading light, it must

accept the blending by which it is
defined. A blue-green box sits beside

me, its color is this place, *Lordship.*
The ashes, bits of bone, tooth, and gold

have settled and a single copper wire
tangled like restlessness loops the adding

and subtracting of how you failed, how I
failed. The brass latch catches the sun's

harsh glare, and one mystery unfolds another:
sawgrass stalks stand like philosophical texts,

act as if they are sawing their way toward
truth, flaunting cattails promenade, and making

no promises, a crane, one leg planted, hoots
a caw-cry. And like those who grieve, it will

soon let go the root, face the blazing sky
and fly over all the long rock and float.

Sisters

Morning sickness is a statement.
I knew this even when my mother's
knitting needles took their cue as she
told the story another way: *A God-given*
gift, each of you, intoned factually
much like: *Today is Saturday; you're*
going to confession. Four sisters. My loose
fingers checked the first, round soft-spot,
slid over the silken hair-threads, made note—
no golden halo. These sisters were objects
without purpose, like souvenirs, wedding
china, details adrift from plot. We grew,
we laughed, played your fault, her fault,
not my fault maybe 100 times, sneered
and sassed our way around Mother's words,
said they lacked substance. We made

tie-dyed shirts, peacocked indigo, turquoise,
and lime, stickered our ceilings, iridescent
stars and moons. One Saturday at High Mass,
I married, and years later, a point beyond
where we set out, a place assuming
an uncertain title, an official order, *Baghdad.*
I watched my husband's face, saw churchless
graveyards, another never-ending war.

Each sister called, said the subject was too big
to pin down. I should fly to New York,
disregard the cold air. The youngest pontificated,
planned (as if she was caring for a lost soul):
we would eat at O' Henry's, attend a play,
meet at St. Pat's, inhale the season's holy scent,
find a patron saint, one who knows how
to contour uncertainty, say a communal prayer,
light five votive candles. Their four sticks,
charred tips buried in the tray's desert-like
sand, stood erect, side by side, next to mine.

Gazing at the Scar

Dear Lena: Today is nothing, another
tepid Tuesday. I took a trip. The doctor
said, *Get outside of yourself; open your
eyes, live.* I'm ashamed. There is so much
dormant energy, and the world is like one
enormous eye, the lashes a fringe between
sky and dark waters. Sometimes I pretend
I'm batty and blind. *Write,* you say, but
inside my head, in all the empty spaces,
there is fear. It rises in the night, hides
behind each half-shut lid, haunts the day,
comes in soft cries. This morning there
was hardly anyone at the museum, only
a handful of workers. A humane woman
with her Wal-Mart-greeter smile (lips
painted cupid-red) poured out cheerful words.
A security guard nodded then rested his
eyes between silence and floors slick
as a surgeon's knife. Up the spiraling stairs,
to the left of all the holy mothers, a hundred
or so it seems, there is a 2 x 4 room. Inside
that womb, the noon light gleamed and brush
strokes (vibrant as blood) spattered the hung
canvas and my mind. Eyes, magic charcoal
circles, seemingly alienated from the painted

head seemed to know my nightmare, and under
the tilt of one eyebrow, deep inside one iris,
a baby hid, complete with shape and breath.
She was a bright young thing. Lena, we never
carry a blank slate; the good or bad move
like threads that loop through the needle's
eye; you know the cold gray unraveling I hide,
the one marked *unwanted child,* the one named
shameful mess. Lena, I want to stop fearing
night's cold crash; I want to slip inside those
suspended eyes, search for some speck
of luminous forgiveness.

Love,
Sister Mary

Words Eating Words

Mothers always know what is best.
I know this is her idea, not mine.

Understand position is everything in life.
I sit straight-backed, knees together.

You must always look pretty.
I fold my hands, bat eyelashes.

Your hair is too curly, looks unruly.
I pull it back, wax all loose ends.

You will take ballet lessons; walk gracefully.
I want to tap, to jingle and click.

Always eat one Christmas pomegranate.
I taste a bitter juice, spit annoying seeds.

Stop daydreaming; listen to what I am saying.
I notice how a fresh wind ruffles the trees.

Oh, the Inconsolable Act

Know. To come upon one's brother as a stone-gray shape
    rolled over, a shadow
waiting to feel the probing
like some old-stone savage,
still breaks wide-open
the night's dead silence.

Understand. Your four fingers
careening between my legs
while the moon's silhouette
slipped all silky through my
open window made real
the no longer wheezing dream.

Listen. When without even one
thought about its everlasting,
spreading entrance, waiting,
and hoping I would grow moist
before light severed the glow,
you emptied all past history
that we were a normal family
(mother, father, sister, brother).

Remember. Always. The moment
when my eyes caught the digging,
your arched back, sweat misting
your forehead, your upper lip, your
hand raking my still young-girl place,
your fingers twisted attachment,
the desire for my ripening, and how
some conversations do recur, how small
flashes can slice slumber and dream.

Hang-Up

Across seven states, across 750 miles,
intrusion is translated into the sound
of my cell phone ringing. Your call,

like morning coffee is ritual on the third
Monday. You say I am your rock. A *rock.*
Something round, something dead cold,

something waiting in the hand ready
to be set sailing across the wave's lick
and lap. A thing thrown under a seagull's

screech and scream. And hearing your
voice the telltale spot circles. How you
entered the night's twilight, my pink

baby doll pajamas, and made real your
desire to disrobe, to touch. I press
the green icon. "Hello." The "o" drawn

long and slow. You tell me you walked
to Savin Rock, had a talk with God.
This is how we pray these days. Nothing

formal like *Hail Mary full of grace;*
Our Father who art in heaven; Bless
me father for I have sinned. Your holy

conversation: "I am far from perfect,
and I have documentation to prove it."
We laugh.

I say I am proud of you; fourteen sober
months, and now transitional housing.
Transition: to change, changeover, move

forward. Across cyber miles, heartfelt
words: *I love you.* I press the red icon,
and while considering the mystery

a passage from my lost childhood
fills the room: *Now I lay me down to*
sleep. I pray the lord his soul to keep.

Algebra I Times 2

His fact-based father-daughter system
was always hard for me to figure out;

everything came in countable sets
and rarely was there a need for celestial

leaps. My report card, with its mustard
envelope parallel, signaled I had created

another alternate angle; the squared box,
the red letter "F" was linked to an impossible

hypothesis. He had charted the course,
even used a slide ruler, had by my birth

owned the theory "x" plus "y" equals you
will be outstanding. I wanted to tell him

we were opposites, like negative and
positive numbers. I wanted to cancel:

his "Can't you see 1 plus 1 equals 2?"
with "I am not you—one number can

replace another." I wanted to subtract him
from me, grow more fatherless each day,

offer as solid proof that seldom are failures
countable and resolutions can be calculated

in imaginary digits (sometimes the word
"imaginary" is the best description

for real numbers). And as my father graphed
more innuendoes, said I would never amount

to anything, I solved the problem, counted out
four words, kept multiplying the set: *Oh* yes *I will.*

August Song

Maimed, but shrewdly deposited, he said:
Some days color binds the soul.
My Inniskeen lover gave me this morsel
of Divine Proportion as he flew around
my head making his iridescent whirlwind.

Peader thought America was like one giant
Crayola box—lift the lid, always a new hue.
On the night we traveled to Carrikatee,
I watched a gray crane with vertical lines

stand by a misty lake; at its mossy bank,
forsythia bushes and wild roses bloomed,
a miniature Aurora Borealis. And beyond
the shining black night, a lopsided Irish

quarter-moon illuminated a tinker's
camp. A redheaded gypsy-girl danced
round and round, and beside her my
grandmother's spirit, like a lost banshee,

moved over mounds of weathered rock
that sprouted hanging fuchsia and long-
legged lavender foxglove. On this night
everything was silvered; I could see

endless fields, Kavanagh's hanging
mountain, hear willows cry. In Dublin,
the whole kit and caboodle dip chips
in curry sauce while Romanian mothers

lined Grafton street; their colorful skirts
catch money, some hammock sleeping
brown-eyed babies. The language they
think in their heads will one day give itself up.

just ask any Irish man or woman passing
under the day's gun-smoke, grieving sky.

He Sits and Rocks Slightly

My father now accepts his mind was lost
at birth, yet some kind of song must
have passed through those gray channels—
this is why he quietly hums *Ave Maria*
at Christmas, why he still prays morning
prayers. And knowing seeds are planted one
by one, he says I am his hero. But fathers
who beat five-year-old sons for leaving
the backyard, for wanting to cross the street,
for wanting, like poets, the joy of a new journey
really believe heroes, like past transgressions,
are manic manifestations, simply a matter
of human position. All phobias are vine tangled,
offer few escape holes, can sometimes even seem
like a profession of faith. Dad's bottom line,
when all else fails, accept God is everywhere,
can gleam on altars, can pace in padded cells,
can melt on your tongue, rise in the holiest of hosts,
can walk in wearing a wide-brimmed straw hat
and denim pants. He carried his world inside
two pockets, and deep inside the right one, the tree
of knowledge sprouted seeds of truth and wisdom.
While the left one, the other one, hid pinpoint
evidence of all his fucked-up faults, and an unraveling
seam where a yellow-eyed owl sits no longer
quite sure how to fly through a moonless night.

III

Her Desire to Bloom

Her Desire to Bloom

I stand next to the Medicine woman,
a myth keeper. Her restless whispering
calls the sun god, rhymes sadness
with dawn; slow notes, sounding like loss,
fly forward then back. Her music
seems to seep from tall pines and sacred
bushes: wood fern, trout lily, squaw root.
Melodic sounds rise over light-hunting
mountains, and the tune mingles with my
unsatisfied need. Last night, I curved my
hand into my husband's hot palm, swung
under his body. Each move filled with visible
pleasure. But still, inside me, nothing grows.

The ancient word falls: *mother*. Each
morning my tongue curls around tribal
prayers, each syllable a sacrifice as I
paint my barren body with the blood-red
powder; I dip (without one restraining thought)
my naked breasts. The frigid black water
channels its way, swirls between legs and thighs.
Yesterday, my plunge brought forth a dove's
deep cooing. The sweet confluence, like need
and desire, coupled my longing. Women,
swinging their rounded hips, place baskets

along the merciless river's edge; the day's
washing overflows. My younger sister
kneels, her swollen breasts waiting for her
baby's suck caress the rubbing stone, a generous,
natural image. I feel envy, but know it is swift
poison, so I rock and sing the old lullabies.
My dream child dwells inside the willow's
shadow; and at night under freezing stars,
I uncurl her ten, tiny, infant fingers.

I Cradle My Daughters

Yesterday, I witnessed how flesh
can part; how chromosomes can branch.

"Horrors at Birth" a show hosted
by a model, one sexy torso, two long,

slender legs, a "Y" reversed. God
can be good even when the expected

is turned upside-down. Her perfect
body leaned toward a woman and two

drowsy toddlers, sisters. Two heads
share one body: chest, heart, stomach,

share one pair of legs, the "Y" upright.
Awareness can silence a hundred wagging

tongues, like when a marksman hits
his target, a mixture of astonishment

and humility (what I saw I struggle
to describe). Beside the mother,

a translator. She moves from Spanish
to English: *My daughters are priceless,*

like communion, a miracle, and never once
do I hear the translator say the words: *"Why me?"*

Vocation

for Mother Mary Rose Therese of the Holy Spirit

Even my dolls smelling of cotton
and plastic, their puffed bellies,
dangling arms, flickering lids,
opening and closing over watchful
eyes, phosphorus as agates, were
seen as needy. Like children learning
to set the table, the fork on the left,
knife on the right, I soon learned
the meaning of words like bless

all daily labor, bless the mercy
of the Lord, bless those who dwell
in hovels, bless the Lord's command
that marks ecclesiastical landscapes
and each God seeker. As a novitiate,
I cut my hair, took my vows: it will be,
and so shall it be. The two fused
like the gray look of the hungry
like the green fullness of the full,
like the fire red of the risk-takers
like the true blue of the peacemakers.

Rippling synapses moved me
from child to adult, a chorus of glittering

voices. A nun is married to His word,
married to the burdens of others,
married to tender expression,
married to the invisible speakers,
married to always giving back.

The Pot Stirrer

When I turn toward the horizon,
there is little color, the sun, the room,
my face, all ash gray. Under the table,
with its cup waiting for the tea's long,
fine-blue whistle, a rough carpet lies
like some old, tawny-haired dog.
I move, half-asleep, under this tired
dome, sit on the unmade bed, prop
first toe then heel, feel the old melody
of the russet-brown, dirt floor—
feel the slow delicate twist as daylight
makes its way, and I push toward
another long peasant's-whey day.
In my village where the sweet sadness
of truth waves its flag, we keep the dyer's
secrets, guard them like delicacies,
recipes that come from cracked mussels
and fingered ink sacks. I tell the children,
"Go, gather whortleberry, anchusa, black
currant." We must make fast and bright
colors—the lovely lavender, bristol red,
gosling green, and mortal sin for queens,

soldiers, and high priests. At the day's end,
I stir the pot, drown the spun, boiled yarn;
and as I watch the piper play his tune, I dream
another perfect-sounding, sad, new color.

Girl in India Is Gravid with Hunger

I was married at twelve; and two years later
my husband, who waited like man's best friend
to bed me, died after shivering sick with sweat
under a noon sun. My mother pushed his pocked
corpse and me into a cart, patted my head, said I
could no longer run among the olive trees or feel
their growing over me. Brash with the fervor of those
who pilfer food, my father left me in a Calcutta
back alley, left me like a leper's bread basket sitting
outside this place. A tall cadaver-like woman,
missing six teeth, four bottom, two top, canines
filed with age, her brown skin a shawl for protruding
bones, opened the door, then pointed to the last empty
space. Someone pushed me, gridlocked stick arms
around my flying and flailing. Later the old woman
showed me a holy book, one full of parables preaching
pulpit wisdom, *Be true to your brothers and sisters;*
blessings upon those who feed the hungry and husbandless
wives. Three women razor-shaved my widow's head, smeared
tamarack paste, and under an indifferent pale moon covered
the bristled hair. Over cement walls, women throw food, dog
scraps, and one month and twenty-four days later, I now follow
the pack and sing with the sister who howls her lunatic cry.

Eruptions from Natural Causes

There are women like me
who have become dormant
volcanoes. They have lost

their roaring, their color,
their triumphant flash; they
are so entirely agreeable. Two

years, and you still say we must
meet inside this cave of blistering
secrets. You say I must be content,

be satisfied with the occasional hot
spots, with your unpredictable solar
system that won't let me surface

as either your sun or moon. I prepare
for another here and there coming.
I have set two plates, and a fire

crackles, the room warms like you
when you swallow my touch.
You want the hot, hard push

that comes after the unbuttoning,
the unsnapping, the unzipping,
the capricious power that comes

with our diverging and converging.
I wonder if you even notice
how I have become a mound

of silence, a smoldering stretching
of discontent as we slide past
one another. Tonight, I polished

and rubbed to a vibrant shine
the low mahogany table, baked
delicate tea cakes, then unwrapped

my grandmother's sake set—each
act, each step, a subtle awareness.
You laugh, say the fire spits

like a woman's anger. I watch how
the pile of ashes glows and then pour
the fragrant Honjozo-shu wine. You

expect the expected, the you-me
molten flowing. But when the last
crumb falls from your mouth, when

the mantle's last candle has been blown
out, I will have cracked wide-open
the thin crusted *you, her, me always-last*

swirl, and welcome the new topography
understanding that when the scorching
lava cools, a new image shapes the earth.

I Used to Know My Name

for Saarjite Baartman

Paper doll figure, hotsie-totsie
girl, everyone knew Barbie's

name. Even with her hair frizzled
and 'froed, legs and arms twisted

to Timbuktu, her prefect waist
turned back to front, front to back,

breast and buttocks viewed
and reviewed; even when dunked

in tubs, dunked in pools, dunked
from tropics to arctics, she always

had a name: *Barbie.* But when Saarjite,
later unwrapped and renamed *Hottentot*

Venus, heard the luscious, vanilla
ice cream *Come with me,* she filled

her lush green world with an I-love-
my-new-dress scream. Her Ken wore

a bone-white lab coat, bone-white
pants; his bone-white face sparked

eyes blue as rolling waves. He pointed,
twisted her head toward the great ship,

said her world, top to bottom, would
be transformed. He led her past the twiggy

stuff of brush, past the men's sideways
glance, up the plank, and when the last

strip of land, the last fluency of color
disappeared, he stripped her young girl

body never saying her name, never saying
Saarjite, only these two words: *Show me.*

Mid-Morning Tea

for Sheri

In the morning's slow holding,
my eyes scarcely look higher
than the milk-toast colored liquid
that pools inside each cup and saucer.
The chemo has turned your stomach;
you wake more tired than the day
before, and today I feel like a stranger
who hides in a misty presence
overseeing conversation.

I speak mostly around what
has happened, as if I could move
beyond this time and place. There
are three straw hairs left on your
head, and in a sideways glance I
count them then circle the room.
Everywhere you are there.

Like the wall's hand-painted border,
red and apple green squares, you
have marked and colored this friendship.
Unraveling time, I want to tell you,
Yesterday I bought a blue jersey,
a boorish blouse, neckline dipped low:

Men like cleavage, a proclamation
from my daughter who is still rooted
in optimism. You stare at my hair and my
eyes move toward your one breast. We
hope for time, time that will convert
this space, a place shared by two friends,
facing too many mirrors, too many fears.

When All Else Fails

after Yousuya Kaidan's "The Story of Oiwa and Tamiya Iemon"

I am a Samurai without a patron,
and more and more I miss, each
day, the crowd's howl and scream,
the hearty clap. It always happens;
what at first is choked in random
thought slowly begins to breathe.
The rich man's daughter, my desire,
my want come together. And needing
so much more, I watch the young girl
dance. Her body bows; her hands,
delicate like lotus flowers, open, point,
beckon. I am like a silky bird that rises,
spirals, then flies toward the window's

light. I told myself over and over
there is no need for heaven's guiding
light, for this was not betrayal. After all,
each night pull myself home, follow
the stars that streak dark skies. Even though
Oiwa is always
too weak to cook,
too weak to clean,
too weak to meet my needs,
I bring my wife red and yellow kimonos,

the finest oilpaper umbrellas. Our infant son
lies beside her, opens one eye, raises
one eyebrow. He seems to know
the names of what I have become,
how I hide behind sweet gestures:
See, each pleat I folded.
They open and close like blinking.

Without Possessions

She'll make her knocking flight . . .
and take wing above the river.
                    Geri Doran

Like a nodding trillium,
head hanging, folding into its pale

self, I slip past all the short-lived
happiness: the five-year, five-layered,

pink-icing birthday cake, the found
kitten at nine, the Garth Brooks tickets,

my one lover. If only my grab and touch
pleased him what follows would not be.

The lines move forward, and I fill a new
form much like spring shapeshifts. I

transform victim into heroine. I am
a child. I paint. My fingers stoke

the canvas wanting to open flowers
and flying skies. I face the now scrubbed

clean architecture, count the you-are-here-
then-you're-gone days, too many what-if

failings. Too many proofs. It's time.
I lift the hung cloak, dyed blue-black

wool, envision slaughtered lambs:
They never could foresee the butchering.

(I must reconstruct the next image.)
My father shook my shoulders once,

the way a nun handles an unknowing
schoolgirl for saying: *Who is God,*

anyhow? A useless question. Forms
grow darker: house, tree branches,

a single flaming azalea, and leaves
like lopsided shrouds swallow minutes.

Upstairs my mother, buttoned inside
her aversion for truth, sleeps. She works

the graveyard shift, reads romance
novels—my mania, another script.

She imagines I am not in danger,
have selves more solid than a star.

Look at what I have become. Look
at me. If only we could reopen our lives

like an abscessed wound, give the past
a chance to heal. Burdened. I divide

my world: bad here, good there, question
how mortality ought to move. I take

a final drag. On cue, my lungs release,
and I saunter past the innocent flock,

their bleating cries, trample blood
virginica, waving clover, claim this spot,

press deep the knife's jagged edge,
and welcome the cold command.

Mouth Music

We were the first mountain singers;
Cherokee women gritty with stamina
who worked unforgiving forests, tilled
rock-filled lands, faced whining cold
north winds, fished the deep black lakes
that had not seen light in three years.
Everyday miracles can rise then quietly
disappear like the trout's big eyes,
can ride on the sweet sound of a sister's
single act. Myrtle-green woods, scrub
pines, scarlet skies knew my need to feed,
heard my painful crawl as I searched out
the plump-bellied fish, fought underwater
boulders, arthritic tree trunks, followed
the notes of animals and ancestors. We
listened to eagles whir, chanted high
and low, danced our fire songs, reeled
in the night light, the shared havoc,
connected like roots, streams, and rivers.

Sonnet in Celebration Of

This is for stunning Sonya and all the other women
with high attitude and victory dripping and bulging
from their fuchsia scar-slashed breasts. For stunning
Sonya who sits rooted among the day's sing-songing,
and proclaims the here-to-there street click-clacking
as church humming—each passerby a silly acronym.

For Sonya, whose husband the poet has a new book
(another hundred thousand words); yet this afternoon,
she cleaned his page under a ceiling ready to bloom
with her very own against-all-odds words. The moon
has seen her arch, has heard her croon like a picayune
insane moment, watched her underscore cancer's hook.

Stand back and you will find on her torso, no tragic flaw.
Yes, stunning Sonya sees it all as the luck of the draw.

Summer Canning

Facing the ruby horizon and a 6 AM
haze, I count out twenty-four glass jars,
one cast-iron pot. Behind me, an old

country song swings and the wood stove's
fire spits its off-beat tune, a far cry from
the field's squawking crows, the tractor,

its roll and jerk, yesterday's rain and wind.
Slicing Jim's harvested tomatoes, the knife
slides down each center-spot, slices through

the thin, delicate membrane. Tiny seeds,
fleshy pieces, and the clear juice puddles
the cutting board counter. The liquid stings

a cut hardly worth my notice. A sudden
knowing can make the ground tremble,
can grow a field of all day rocking back

and forth, can crow the need to color what
is known invisible. A slam and a face filled
with the sound of *the world will never be*

the same slaps wide-open the screen
door. Let me say exactly each word: "Jim fell
under the thresher, was slashed limb-to-limb."

My lungs took the weight, my right hand grabbed
the table's corner. The pot spits boiling droplets,
six immersed jars rattle, and one slowly cracks.

Before the Peril of Unconsciousness

Inside an imploding corner, hands knotted,
a young mother hunts for a way out, inhabits
two states: I want to live, and I want the end
to happen now. One child is playing checkers,
another is dancing round and round and round.
And as she cleans each room, dusting shelves
and tables, she hums a few old songs. Then
quick like a kick to the shin or an elbow to a rib,
she rewrites the tailored script that a good mother
is a milk and honey trip. Upstairs, the youngest
wakes and cries the word *Momma.* She see-saws
between its righteous tic and tock, then calls,
Bath time. She kneels on the unsteady ground,
ignores the mirrored image, the bobbing, all
lucid thoughts, the claw, the last tug, each child's
wild-eyed stare, each child's last gulp for air.

IV

In God's Hands

In God's Hands

We kneel. We drag her in to burn votives
and she's so thin candlelight passes through her . . .
                                        Erin Batykefer

I

Wednesday at Rosewood's coffee shop
I see an old friend: *You look great. So*
do you. Where does time go?

II

Mary Kate lives in Charleston,
is expecting her second. Steven
tried three years to adopt. Elle,
the queen of broken hearts, is gay:
San Francisco is easier, for her.

III

Colin finishes this year. He is frenzy-locked, waiting
not knowing.

IV

Clearance special.
Red-bowed gardenias
creamy pungent flowers curl like well-kept secrets.
Reduced for Quick Sale

V

Then her husband. *Mickey is a user.*
Cocaine. For years. Lake house,
Lincoln, Colin's college fund, her life
snorted up each bulging nostril.

VI

Fran scribbles her new number
on a folded, blank bank deposit-slip,
begs me to pray a rosary for Steven.

VII

She takes a deep breath.

Her Life at the Border

on the train to Dundalk

. . . and here it is: in a voice no louder
than the whisper that a dipper's wing
makes ruffling water, the mother prays

while the father, coarse and dirty,
makes hay inside days that battle
intermittent gray-dawn light;

and as she rocks tight-hearted, keeping
faith beside the lavender sea, her fingertips
count the rosary's push and pull and drag

with each sorrowful mystery the idea
that God forgives. And in a backward
glance between her to and fro, she counts

the hillside sheep, the times the traveler
whistled, the times he softly called her name,
the times when dawn meant she would

feel the moving of his hands from her
face, to breast, to thigh and their gypsy
screams under suspended clouds. These

moments of her and him, their naked
truth, are now the shadow that lives
deep inside the field's crumbling hedge.

Adoration

Lower Salt Hill and I sit
waiting for the #2 bus.

An old woman with steel-wool
curls wears a tailored suit

and a white silk blouse. Her hose,
much darker than *Nude,* adds

dignity to her black nun-shoes.
I sit beside her, slouched, lost

in a mid-day daydream. I stand,
move with grace and conscious

thought, tug at my candy-cane
halter. A girl knows when she

looks good, when she can sing
a map-green ocean. In the distance,

the cathedral bell rings, splinters
the sea-soaked air: "Do you know

what time ...?" The words are
hushed mid-sentence. The woman

moves a gnarled finger to her lips.
It is the Angelus hour. Obedient, I cast

my eyes in prayer, and between each
Hail Mary's fill and fall I meditate

then remember the crowded streets'
clang, the bartender's massed forearms,

the church alley, the ecstasy of a half-moon
and the kiss that brought me to my knees.

Regarding Her Rival

Though not humped, limped,
toothless, or brainless, I feel

inevitably maimed: my flesh sags,
my forehead bears the mark

of bewilderment, my eyes the dark
shadows of self-loathing. And he

who once held out an offering hand,
one longing, one desiring the triumph,

one needing the harvest, seeks no longer
my breasts, the moist parting, the turn on,

the throb, the high inflate of titillation
subsumed, the iridescent love-making

transcending jealousy. Then declaring
youth, another replaced me like magenta

sunsets replace the day's yellow glow.
Stunning entrances flaunt her lastingness,

her probing tongue, her slender thighs
that swing and sing, her climactic consumer

goods. And on growing old: I can still
bend, flex most muscles, can change

according to most circumstances,
and my name is still Amelia. Things

can change, can even disappear, except
this everlasting vigilant spite that curses

her tight buttocks, her slender thighs,
and her unblemished come-to-me body.

Melina's Vigil

Four forty-five. Hypnotized by the boiling
noodles that float like torn pieces of flesh,
I think how bad my feet ache; how I want
to leave my skin. *It would be nice to have
a new one, shiny satin with pearl buttons.*

The baking bread's warmth circulates,
and I remember my father's cold-hearted
words: *This is business.* Bankrolls, liras
stacked one on top of the other. My parents
gave me away, no, sold me, without even

one, "Do you love him?" For thirty-two years
this marriage has stalked, stabbed, dismembered
any hope of caring. Halfway across the room
Virgillio sits naked from the waist up; half alive
I move from room to room, from floor to bed,

from each tug, pet, lick, roll, and ejaculated
grunt. I follow his daily command, push
the cellar door; it screeches like a hurt bird.
Cases of beer are banked in shadows like my
letters from a long-ago lover. I unfold one,

the words bring comfort like daily prayer. One
slow breath rolls into another. Down here my
life is never sullied; I hold my head high before
making the ritualistic haul up the mottled, mossy
steps. My back aches, but consumed by the fight
to win, I chant: *I will outlive him! I will. I will.*

Against the Tide of Asceticism and in Awe of Midday Dreams

after viewing Dale Chihuly's Seaform Loop #2

To endow their blown fluency
my mind imagines Hama's waters
how they can hide magnificent

white snakes and seaforms. How
giant conch shells, moment by moment
swallow sins from eight billion lifetimes.

This one lies still as looking-glass
until my desire for more, a sudden
need for more, signals change.

Then it rises, shakes a burning salt spray,
struts moving long tangerine and lemon
tentacles. I have always loved my

daydreams, the swirl of faces, the sea
of voices, the witnessing of a good story,
one that holds life together like capillaries

stringing their way to all the body's furthest
outposts. Now the vein of this preposterous
untruth takes another turn. A passing nymph

asks me to dinner. I accept, settle on a black
silk dress, red-lipped glass slippers. I didn't
mind the first course, a seaweed salad

or the bearded guy with a patch over one
eye sitting on my right. I loved the endless
pale scallops—their pattern of circles

on a broken, blue china plate. I gobbled
my fearless love for thunder and fast-moving
currents, and the swimming questions:

Shall I forget someday I will grow old?
Shall I wrap myself in coral pinks,
a girl's face? Shall I take as my own this

new-found buoyancy, sustain the brewing,
ignore the briny taste of too many yesterdays,
succumb to this new nibbling: *Never look back?*

When We Cannot Wash Shame Like Soiled Sheets

I. Winter

My bedroom door creaks, and I
wait *to serve, to please.* His words
blur like something passed through
memory: *Spring's first snake still
sleeps.* Strange words. The fire
cracks, and he unties my gown;
we are like linen and lace, form
a strong bond. Under satin sheets,
I feel his great majesty, hear two
winter-wrens sing. All men, gods
or not, fear cold-blooded women
and cold beds. Exhausted, we part.

II. Spring

Plum trees open, bud
one plum then another, branch
and leaves bend low. I have
turned half-green wishing to see
him, all of him. Jonquils lift their
heads, and I tell him that I dreamt
that he pretends sleep, lives inside
a netherworld; the eelgrass nods
when we pass. He laughs. Always
respectful, I bow and hand him
a stitched white-tongued lotus
garland. Three times he fingers
the gift, and the third time he reaches
for me. A ravine opens, spouts water.
When the first cock crows, I am alone.

III. Summer

I watch, like a crow perched,
his shadow climb, inch its way
toward Mount Mimoro, slither
across rocks. Sweet Jasmine curls
round the pagoda—look at the flowers!
I walk past rice fields, workers' bent
backs, a tall patch of weeds hiss.
The noon sun burns my skin; a farmer
offers a drink, cold water from a mountain
spring. He tells me to watch my step.

IV. Autumn

Leaves shrivel and the lush
gardens shed their green skins.
The harvest moon brings light.
His eyes soften, meet mine and his arm
coils around my waist; his hold is tight.
Still, when the sun unwinds the morning
I am left with one chair, one bowl. I swallow
deep breaths, and write on rice paper:
I long to see you, all of you.
I wait, wait, wait . . .
October winds snake and twist a growing
willow's branches. My bedroom window
catches the day's breaking light as my
husband slides through my unfinished
sleep. His body sways back and forth.
I am a hollow briefly filled with touch
and sound. Before leaving, he unfolds
my note, then writes: *My young wife, most
of our great world remains a dark secret.*

V. Winter Returns

I set the breakfast table (steamed
rice and grilled fish), braid my
glistening hair, twist three gold
star-pins, and turn the door's
brass latch. One missed period,
and now morning sickness. My
hands, sensing upheaval, hold
the sink. Things always reveal
themselves by shape and sound.
A hiss, a tongue flickers, a blur
of a blur returns. Peeling layers,
shedding skin, clutching a world
unknown to me, my husband stands:
snake, human, myth. My scream,
blood red if it had a hue, shatters
this private space. And with his
giant, viper-head bowed, he winds
past me, leaves our home, then
crosses Seta Bay. Ice coats a bare
plum tree, a branch snaps. I feel

an uncoiling and grab the kitchen's
sharpest knife, grip the handle, swing
high then low, stab womb then chest.
A red-crowned crane blinks.
Winter's first snow falls.

Judgment Day

for P.D.

I am still so fearful of the heaven or hell
moment, the bad against good: the stolen
five dollar bill, the times I lied to save
my own skin, the knowledge of betrayal,
the oblivious discarded vows to love
and honor, all my tales of love and squalor.
The human form can be corrupt, but at some
point we all long for another chance,
and another, and another. I know punishment
is due, yet sometimes a small pant of light
breaks over my right shoulder and I wonder
if heaven is a place where crimson-robed
souls trumpet everlasting forgiveness.
I want to be generous, religiously send
gold-faced Mass cards; my often-locked
mind questions Purgatory, questions
if each transgression matters? I am sure hell
is a fire-pit, not one green blade or the ruckus
of cattails, is a vortex of charred tree trunks,
is a place where the devil and all dirty men must
dwell. I now care for my ailing mother, lift her
in and out: bed, chair, toilet, chair, bed, toilet,
and yesterday I refused to let one of God's
creations, a snake plant, with its flame-licking

stalks, die. I try to hold, as truth, the Savior's
tomb was, the third day, empty. But I have
entered death's space, a place less than agony;
a time when urgency to move between this
and that is not so far-reaching, have seen
when the soul must turn, leave hindsight,
follow the assigned path, it is veiled
in a holy state and ceases to wonder about
words like *blame* and *direction*.

Notes

"Gazing at the Scar"—after *Head,* by Alfred Henry Mauer

"He Sits and Rocks Slightly"—after *Seeking,* by Jonathan Green

"The Pot Stirrer"—after *The Cloth Dyers,* anonymous

"Eruptions of Natural Causes"—after *Pillars Sake Set,* Pillars Pottery

"Her Desire to Bloom"—after *Medicine Woman,* by Nancy Horn Wagner

"I Used to Know My Name"—after *Hottentot Venus Tribute: Barbie Marathon,* by Dawn Hunter

"Mouth Music"—after *Upper Creek Summer,* by Jim Crompton

"To Hell with Cupid"—after *Hej duk,* by Ursula Von Rydingsvard

"In God's Hands"—after *Flowering Tornado,* by Ginny Ruffner

"Sonnet in Celebration Of"—after *Nude Torso,* by Marjorie Hinman Craft

"Against the Tide of Asceticism and in Awe of Mid-day Dreams"—after viewing Dale Chihuly's *Seaform Loop #2*

"Summer Canning"—after *Mountain Woman,* by Jim Crompton

"When We Cannot Wash Shame Like Soiled Sheets"—written after research that included reading *Japanese Ghosts and Demons: Art of the Supernatural,* edited by Stephen Addiss

CPSIA information can be obtained at www.ICGtesting.com
Printed in the USA
LVOW042148150412

277684LV00006B/3/P